1. Athens
2. Australia
3. China
4. Israel
5. Belarus
6. Austria
7. Switzerland
8. Germany
9. Italy
10.

Olympic Movement (Sport
                    Culture
                    Equipment

THE ISLAND OF MAUI

A Photographic Journey

PHOTOGRAPHY BY
Howie From Maui®
Erik Aeder
Michael S. Nolan

WRITTEN BY
Gaia Rettinghouse, M.A.

DESIGNED BY
Helen Milne

EDITED BY
Nancy J. Halley

Aerial photography made possible by Alex Air.

A photographer is a visionary

He is an expert at timing and at visioning

He offers us a gift of beauty

His photographs make statements

More powerful than words

We can view his moment of perfection

Time and time again

We can enjoy his vision which is "captured"

And by so being, is now freely shared

We look upon it, as whole

He viewed it through the lens

His focus is our gift

Which is also his reward.

CONTENTS

The Island of Maui - A Photographic Journey
© By Howie From Maui, Inc. ®

First Edition, April 2001

ISBN: 0-9710480-0-2

Produced by
Howie From Maui, Inc.®
P.O. Box 1179
Kula, Hawaii 96790
808-874-5449
Toll-free: 888-Moonbow (666-6269)
www.howiefrommaui.com

Printed in Singapore

Gaia Rettinghouse M.A.
I have enjoyed adding verse and text to this lovely photographic journey
of Maui. I have traveled the world because of my love for beauty in nature.
All places of natural beauty are sacred. Being on Maui is like dreaming
without boundaries. Maui is my home.

ALOHA AND WELCOME TO MAUI

Come along on a journey with us to the most beautiful places on Maui.
Sit back, get comfortable, and enjoy every breathtaking view, every peaceful valley,
every refreshing waterfall, and all the gifts of nature that Maui so generously gives to us,
for the pure pleasure of our enjoyment.

Without the use of colored filters or computer enhancements, all these
inspiring photographs are natural, unaltered images.

Our journey includes Maui's beautiful and sacred places, places only accessible by aerial
views, and places such as Jaws that most of us will only experience through these amazing
feats of photography.

Your voyage is by air, land, and sea.

Our intention is to bring you the best of Maui through the expert eyes of three
photographers, who know Maui and her pristine surrounding ocean waters intimately.

You are about to visit places on Maui that your spirit and heart already know and love.

Through this photographic journey you can return to the island of Maui time and time
again, to enjoy her lovely visions.

~ Gaia Rettinghouse

North Shore Coastline

HOWIE FROM MAUI

by Air and Land ®

Haleakalā Sunrise
January 1, 2000

North Kihei Sunset

Maui allows her cadence
to rest upon us
Her nature, to unearth us
Her truth, to reveal itself to us
Her wisdom, to pour through us

Her aloha is whispered
Gently to us

Her spirit is given freely to us
Her silence speaks through us
Her colors embrace us
And we find ourselves home

Kihei Coastline

Maui is one of the most beautiful tropical islands in the world. She is a world class vacation destination and home to some of the most beautiful beaches found on our planet.

Maui is the second youngest and second largest of the Hawaiian island chain, with an area size of 728.8 sq. miles. There are 120 miles of coastline.

More remote than any other place on Earth, Maui is loved for her year-round sunshine. Maui's weather is determined more by where you are on Maui than by what time of year you are there.

Maui is home to the largest dormant volcano in the world, Haleakalā Crater, which is also Maui's only national park. Haleakalā Crater is 10,023 feet tall. If you add on 20,000 feet or so lying under the sea, it is one of the tallest mountains on Earth. Many visit Haleakalā Crater to watch the sunrise or view the famous silversword plant that is an endangered species.

Maui is not only culturally diverse, retaining her love for hula dance, traditional luau feasts, and blessing ceremonies, she is geographically diverse as well.

West Maui is the location of historical Lahaina town, with its busy harbor and beautiful West Maui Mountains. Just above Lahaina is the resort area of Ka'anapali and north of that is beautiful Kapalua.

Kihei Sunset

In Central Maui is the county seat of Wailuku, the taking off point to enter into 'Iao Valley, a state park. The refreshing area of 'Iao Valley has been a sacred place since ancient times. 'Iao in Hawaiian means, "supreme light".

Upcountry Maui is cooler than the lower coastal areas. It is home to natural herb and flower farms. The slow paced town of Makawao, lovely Kula with her botanical gardens, and the entrance into Haleakalā can be found there.

On Maui's north shore is Pai'a, a small township and popular place for surfers. Leaving Pai'a and heading east on Hāna Highway, the road begins its 500 plus curves and turns and 54 one lane bridges, which wind through a tropical rainforest and pass numerous lush waterfalls.

South Maui is known for its beautiful beaches and snorkeling reefs. Off South Maui shores, Molokini Crater is visible. Molokini is a favorite spot for snorkelers and divers alike and considered one of the top dive spots in the world. The town of Kihei is one of the fastest growing townships in the world lined with many condos and lovely white sand beaches.

Maui has thousands of repeat visitors who come as often as they can and many live here part of the year. It is a relaxed heavenly paradise enjoyed by all who live here and visit.

Wailea golf courses

Molokini sunset

We look out beyond the shores of South Maui
there is Molokini in sight
A crescent shaped cinder cone moon
that brings snorkelers pure delight.

With its shallow reef and array of tropical fish
even a sanctuary for birds,
This marine reserve will remain
One of the prettiest places in the world.

Molokini and the West Maui Mountains

Little Beach sunset

13

North Kihei sunset

Mākena sunset

Mākena with Big Island in the background

15

Sunsets
Give closure to the day
An array of colors
Over the Pacific waters
Make such a beautiful display

Looking out at the horizon
The sun will melt into the sea
She slips into the waters
And becomes a memory

She takes her nightly dip
And vanishes from sight
And we are left to welcome
The coming of the night

Kihei Sunset

Little Beach, Mākena

Little Beach and Big Beach, Mākena

Big Beach, Mākena, with the West Maui Mountains in the background.

'Iao Valley

'Iao Valley to Lāna'i

'Iao Valley
Lush green valley
Cools us

Refreshing waters
Soothe us

Deep cut
Clouded mountains
Renew us

20

At right 'Iao Stre.

'Iao Valley to Haleakalā

'Iao Needle

'Iao Valley to Wailuku

Wall of Tears, 'Iao Valley

23

Haleakalā Crater

Haleakalā sunrise

Kapalaoa cabin Haleakalā National Park

Sunrise
Sends her rays of light
High above the clouds
Bringing the morning in quietly
From the night
Then slowly lighting up the sky
From the darkness of the night

Haleakalā sunrise

Haleakalā sunrise

27

Haleakalā, West Maui Mountains, Molokaʻi and Oʻahu

28

Haleakalā sunrise

Haleakalā Crater

On a clear morning
Above the clouds,
We see the Big Island of Hawaiʻi
In the distance

Here from Haleakalā
The house of the sun
We can enjoy the sunrise
And the sunset

Mysterious cinder cones
This huge dormant volcano
As close to heaven
As we can be

Sitting here
Above it all
Nature's quiet place
Of harmony

West Maui mountains

West Maui Mountains

Colors of the Rainbow

First bright
Then more subdued

Colors of the rainbow
Double delight
Pleasure renewed

Double colored rainbows
Are a treat in paradise
So many colors of the rainbow
Archway of lights
Sweeping across Maui's
Lovely skies

Kapalua

Ka'anapali Beach sunset

Ka'anapali

Lahaina Harbor

Ho'okipa

North Shore

Pā'ia Beach and town

Baldwin Beach

Hāna

MAUI NATURE

Maui allows her cadence to rest upon us
Her nature, to unearth us
Her truth, to reveal itself to us
Her wisdom, to pour through us

Her aloha is whispered
Gently to us

Her spirit is given freely to us
Her silence speaks through us
Her colors embrace us
And we find ourselves home

Road to Hāna

Hāna waterfall

Red Sands Beach, Hāna

Hāna is a song of the soul
Hāna is her waterfalls
And her forests so green
Hāna is a quietude
Of solitude supreme

Heavenly garden of paradise
Remote haven of peace
Hāna is natural beauty
As natural as natural can be

Hāna is her people
Generations of Hawaii's past
Hāna is the sound of silence,
A silence that will last

Kula

At the end of every sunset
Our senses stay alert
For that brief, spontaneous moment
When a green flash can be observed.

I have rarely seen one
In a quick moment they are gone,
But this one caught the last ray of light
And continued on and on.

At left Green flash, Kula

Moonbow made of magic
Rainbow colored light,
Showing itself to us
Amidst the darkness of the night.

Moonbow "Night Rainbow"

Double rainbow, Ulupalakua

45

Pete Cabrinha, Jaws

ERIK AEDER

Maui Wave Sports

Mike Waltze, Jaws

Rush Randle, Jaws

Surfing Jaws is an enormous experience. For these guys it's not a lifestyle, its their lives.

Surfing is a part of ancient Hawaiian tradition.
Hawaiians made surfboards from breadfruit trees, koa trees, and the prized Wiliwili trees. These boards were heavy, sometimes weighing 200 lbs.

Surfing Jaws is as challenging as it is rewarding.
The exhilaration they experience and the victory of coming through
the other side of the barrel, or shooting on through the tube, is one that few of us will ever know.

These guys are not conquering nature, they are joining her powerful forces and going along skillfully for the ride. They are in it for the high. You can only imagine the adrenaline rush that comes from this extreme sport.

The night before a huge swell, it is hard for most surfers to sleep, laying awake anticipating what Jaws may have in store the next day.

These guys are first rate athletes who's mind, body, and spirit need to be one when they join up with sets of waves at these proportions.

Even though the mind and body are prepared, there are still calculated risks involved.

Their lifestyle has to be spontaneous, ready at any time for mother nature's beckoning call.

Courageous and prepared, they set out across the pineapple fields with anticipation.

Surfing is less of an individual sport today as it was. At Jaws, these guys know they need each other.

Safety comes first and many have risked their lives to help each other.

The waves at Jaws can have a sixty foot face on them. It's hard to imagine what that would feel like, taking off in front of a thundering wall of water in motion. There is a respect for the power of the ocean that is equal to none.

Brett Lickle, Jaws

Brett Lickle, Jaws

Darrick Doerner, Jaws

Lloyd Ishimine, Honolua Bay

You're trusting
You're breathing
It's a natural
It's "The High"

You're elated
You're intoxicated
By the wind, wave, and sky.

Fred Vern, Windmills

Buzzy Kerbox, Jaws

A zest for life
An excitement
The thrill of an enormous wave
Pushing from behind
Towering over
Challenges even the bravest

... meets the challenge
... stays ahead of the game
...rides the excitement
...moves with the wind
...takes it to the limit

Darrick Doerner, Jaws

Mike Waltze, Jaws

Luke Hargreaves, Jaws

Dave Kalama, Jaws

56

Dave Kalama, Jaws

Surfers, Honolua Bay

57

Buzzy Kerbox, Jaws

Mike Waltze, Jaws

58

Rush Randle and Pete Cabrinha

Darrick Doerner, Jaws

Pete Cabrinha and Mark Angulo, Jaws

59

Rush Randle, Jaws

You've paddled out and found your spot
You've chanted the wind chant
Given from the ancient days
The waves can pound you!

You stay in front,
Low and ahead
Moved by the forces of nature
You breathe
With concentration and grace.
Agile and steadfast,
You are fully committed.

You will move with this force
More than a flow
The slapping, roaring of the wave
Breathes life into you.

You're now breathing the force of that flow,
While the wind and the wave take you home.

Rush Randle, Jaws

Rush Randle, Jaws

Gerry Lopez, Jaws

Robert Teriitehau, Jaws

Rush Randle, Jaws

Lisa Cabrinha, North Shore

Gerry Lopez, Mākena

65

Becky Lavalla and Alyson Lopez

Mike Stewart, Jaws

Pete Cabrinha, Jaws

Dave Kalama, Jaws

There is a passion for excitement that can take
one over the edge. You never return the same.
Actually, in truth, you never really return.

Robby Seeger, Jaws

Jason Polakow, Jaws

Sierra Emory, Jaws

Robbie Naish, Jaws

Tiare, Nāpili

It's speed, it's precision
It's courage, it's stance,
It's life on the edge,
A most powerful romance.

Elise Garrigue, Honolua Bay

Julie Prochaska, Kanahā

Natalie Asturi, Kanahā

Sierra Emory, Jaws

Threatening, tremendous,
treacherous, tumbling,
terrifying, thundering thrills.

Arnd, Ho'okipa

71

Rush Randle, Kanahā

Albert Jenks and friend

Sean Ordonez, Ho'okipa

Elliot Lebou, Kanahā

Matt Kinoshita, North Shore

Bobby and Anna, North Shore

Humpback whales

MICHAEL
Maui Marine Life
NOLAN

Spinner dolphins

Humpback whale

Previous page: Hawaiian monk seal

The Pacific oceans surround our beautiful island of Maui.

One hundred and twenty miles of beaches encircle us.
The living ocean is vibrant and uncontained.

Within these warm, protected waters live spinner, bottlenose,
and spotted dolphins.
Dolphin are abundant and can be easily enjoyed on a snorkeling trip to the
island of Lāna'i, which is part of Maui county.
They are also playing in the waters off South Maui, near Mākena Beach, or
La Perouse Bay and although protected by the Harassment Act,
snorkelers are known to get in the waters and swim with them.

The Hawaiian humpback whales migrate to Maui in October and stay until early spring.
During their time on Maui they are fasting. While they are here, they mate or
give birth to their calves.

People travel from all over the world to be on Maui during this time, not only to get
away from the cold climates they live in, but to observe the humpback whales
with their variety of behaviors.
Whale watching on Maui is one of her major attractions. There is nothing
more exciting than to watch a breaching humpback whale!

Hawaiian green sea turtles are plentiful on Maui. One well known place to see them is Turtle
Town off the shoreline of South Maui. You can also view them from the boats coming in and
out of Ma'alaea Harbor.

The warm waters and reefs of Maui are home to a wide variety of tropical
fish, making Maui a snorkeler's paradise.

The Hawaiian monk seal is a solitary creature who remains on the endangered species
list. Scientists consider the Hawaiian monk seal to be a living fossil.

Finally, the whale shark, with its distinctive markings, is the largest of the fishes. Very little is
known about its natural history or biology.

Maui is an ocean lovers paradise and home to thousands of marine species playing in her seas
and living within her coral reefs.

Humpback whale

There is no other experience
Like watching the Hawaiian
Humpback whale breach.

You are staring out at the vast
Expanse of the sea and
Leaping up from its depths
A forty-five ton whale emerges,
Catapulting into the air!

Its deliriously exhilarating
Nothing can compare.

FEMALE HUMPBACK WHALES

She is calm and watchful,
Protective and serene.
She is the gentle giant,
Poised,
Moving slowly throughout the seas.

The males fight to be her first choice.
She'll choose the strongest,
Giving her unborn the best.
While the competition goes on around her,
She's basically unimpressed.

Humpback whale

Humpback whale

Humpback whale, mother and calf

Spinner dolphins

Dolphins delight us
Show us the way,
Back to our playful nature

Spinning and turning
Frolicking and gay,

Friendly dolphins
In the water,
Invite us in to play!

Spinner dolphins

Spinner dolphins

Hawaiian Monk Seal

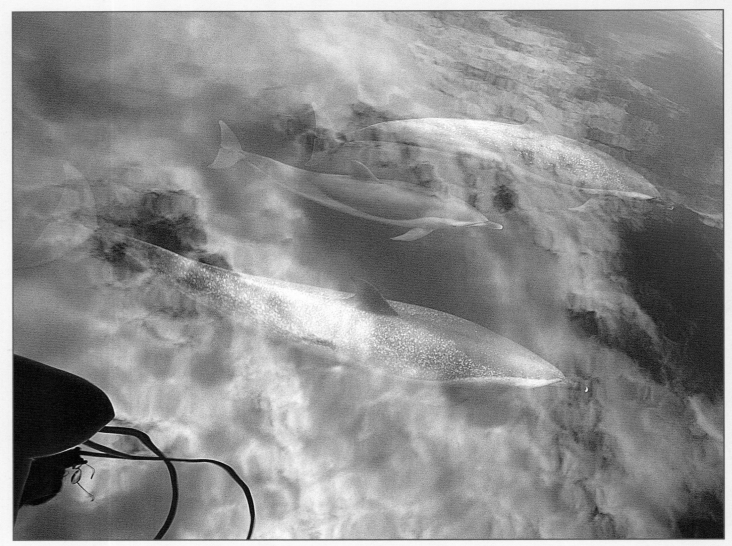
Spotted dolphins

Humpback whale

Humpback whale

A monumentous sound,
The Hawaiian humpback whale
Breaches
With a power so strong!

Tremendously moving,
Water sprays all around
The splashing explosion of the humpback,
Resounds!

Humpback whale

Humpback whale

It leaves us in wonder:
It moves unrestrained,
The mystery of the humpback
Cannot be explained!

Hawaiian bottlenose dolphins

Hawaiian bottlenose dolphins

Spinner dolphins

Spinner dolphins

White tip shark

White tip shark

Hawaiian sea turtle

Hawaiian sea turtle

Whale shark

The whale shark
Moving stealthy through the water
It's massive size and spotted markings
Belie its calm demeanor.

Whale shark

If you want to know your intuition

Take a boat from Ma'alaea Harbor

and listen to the seas

Listen for the humpback's song

Listen to the breeze

Listen to the wind line

Alert, yet at ease

Humpback whale